DEAD
TRUE CRIME

3

POISON
WIDOW

Arsenic Murders in the Jazz Age

C.J. MARCH

SLINGSHOT
BOOKS

Chicago, 1919

I n March 1919, Chicago was enjoying a lull. The last strains of "Over There" and "Keep the Home Fires Burning" wafted out of the city's vanishing saloons as native sons and daughters came home from Europe, many limping, many in pine boxes. The First World War, with its sixteen million dead, had ended only four months before. Chicago's GIs had come home just in time for the great influenza epidemic that would kill nearly five percent of the world's population, but by March, that too had blown out of the Windy City. Not until September would Shoeless Joe Jackson and his White Sox teammates shame Chicago by throwing the World Series in a gambling scheme. The race riots of the summer, women's right to vote, and the beginning of Prohibition, which would make the consumption of alcohol illegal for more than a decade, were all still to come that year. It was a pretty good time for a wedding.

Frank Kupczyk and Tillie Ruszkakski had only been courting five days, but with life so uncertain, why wait? The marriage came just five weeks after the death of Tillie's second husband, who had died shortly after they were married. At a different time, perhaps this knowledge would have given Frank pause, but with one of every four people in Chicago having had symptoms of the lethal flu, death was no stranger. The couple moved into an apartment on North

Winchester Avenue in the Polish area of Chicago and settled into married life.

A couple of years went by. Each day, Frank would leave at 6 a.m. to work at a mop factory. Every night, he came home to Tillie's dinners. But sometime in the spring of 1921, another man started paying Tillie visits after Frank left in the morning. A neighbor, a gravedigger for All Saints Cemetery, saw Tillie kiss this new man. When she suspected she was being observed, she covered the windows with newspapers. Frank must have been surprised to find the view blocked when he got home that night. What reason Tillie gave him is anyone's guess.

When Frank fell suddenly and seriously ill, Tillie wasted no time preparing for his funeral. She sat next to his bed, "calmly sewing her mourning hat and dress," while Frank writhed and weakened. She let neighbors know that "he would not live long." Tillie had a gift for knowing when someone was going to die.

Poland had its own history of witches, and there have been *Szeptucha* (a kind of female Orthodox Christian healer, literally, "Whisperer") in parts of Poland for generations. Tillie's neighbors knew that her "sight" was a far more fearsome proposition; she wasn't healing anybody.

"My man, he's got only two inches to live," she told her landlady, Martha Wesolek. "But for you, boska, you got eight inches to live." The landlady was right to construe that as a veiled threat; her tenant was someone she and the neighbors had learned not to cross.

Tillie went coffin shopping and bought one "at a bargain" for $30. She showed Frank the coffin sale advertisement, proud of her "economic prowess." Wesolek brushed off her request to store it in the basement. "I chase you and the coffin out." The landlady was worried, though. When she visited Frank later, she watched Tillie laugh as he lay dying.

Tillie said she was going to wear the hat she was making to his funeral. The same hat she would end up wearing at her own trial.

Tillie's threats may have worked, because the landlady finally gave her permission to store the coffin, not in the basement, but right in the apartment. And lest Frank have any doubt, Tillie "assured her husband that his illness would be fatal." Frank's face was "swollen, the color of chalk. Each breath he drew racked his emaciated body with almost unendurable pain." Tillie refused to call a doctor and wouldn't let neighbors get one.

She correctly predicted Frank's death to the day, boosting her reputation as a fortune-teller in the neighborhood. He took his last labored breath on April 25, 1921. Tillie had taken away his pillows to hasten his end. As the body grew cold, she grabbed the corpse by the ear and shouted, "You devil, you won't get up any more." Then she cranked the Victrola and played jazz loudly in the apartment.

The death certificate listed the cause as bronchial pneumonia, a common and killing complication during the flu epidemic. But this was a different kind of scourge. More than a few Chicagoans would die an agonizing death before this plague was arrested. When Frank Kupszyk's body was exhumed a year later, the coroner's chemist would find enough arsenic in his organs to kill four men.

N eighbors passed along the street under the shadows of the buildings and greeted one another with *Proszę, Proszę*; some stopping to buy sausages with names like *Metka* and *Śląska*, and *Parówki*. There were over 320,000 Polish immigrants living in Chicago. The neighborhoods were known by many names, including "Little Poland," "Little Warsaw," and "Back of the Yards"; the last from their proximity to the famous Chicago stockyards, where many found work. From the 1850s to the 1920s, Polish immigrants flocked to the city in an influx called *Za chlebem*, meaning "For bread."

Confronted with the cultural differences of an industrial America, "onetime farmers, now Polish American workers, sought to create a society similar to the one they left behind." Self-reliant and industrious, the Polish immigrants created an enduring home in Chicago, built on church, community, and family.

By 1922, though, the Chicago crime scene was hot. The country was getting used to the Volstead Act, the nationwide constitutional ban on the "production, importation, transportation, and sale of alcoholic beverages"—a.k.a. a perfect business opportunity for the criminal underground. And the Chicago Crime Commission, a watchdog group of businessmen, had its eye squarely on the Chicago Outfit, the crime syndicate that operates in the city to this day. The commission managed to reduce the "clogged condition of the criminal court dockets" which "constituted a serious deterrent to the war on organized crime." In 1930, this group of business leaders—not the authorities—introduced the Public Enemy list. Chicago gangster Al Capone was the first Public Enemy Number One. Later, the FBI would adopt this idea in the form of the Ten Most Wanted list. But in the run-up to 1922, another crime scare had been sweeping the city; one that Tillie, soon to be known by the last name of her last victim, Klimek, would play her part in spreading.

Tillie had been in the United States most of her life, emigrating from Poland with her parents in the 1870s when she was still a young child. The family lived and worked in "Little Warsaw," part of the close-knit Polish community. Tillie's childhood was all work and "no foolishness." At the tender age of fourteen, Tillie was married to her first husband, Joseph Mitkiewicz. The details of her early adulthood and her marriage to this first Joseph are lost. She may have had aspirations of buying a tailor shop.

Chicago tenement neighborhood, 1920.

In the neighborhood, she became known for a couple of things. The first was her excellent cooking. The second was her predictions of the deaths of those around her. And the people around her *did* die—husbands, neighbors, children, dogs. Invariably, those who died had argued with her or done something she didn't like.

Her first husband died in January 1914. She received $1,000 in insurance money. After the death of Joseph Mitkiewicz, she remarried within a few weeks. On February 14, she married John Ruszkakski, but he would not see another Valentine's Day. In May, he too died. Ruszkakski is said to have left $2,000 in insurance. Within just a few months, Tillie had significantly increased the cash in her sugar bowl.

Soon she met the man she wanted for husband number three. Guszkowski's first name was either John or Joseph: her string of beaus included a number of Johns and Josephs and the newspapers found it difficult to keep them straight. The two took a trip to Milwaukee using some of the insurance money from the death of her second husband. But during this trip, she made an admission that soured Guzkowski's matrimonial interests.

Tillie, maybe in a gesture of confidence (or threat), told him she'd killed her first two husbands. Reasonably, Guzkowski decided that he didn't want to marry Tillie after all. She met his refusal with blackmail: if he told anyone about the murders, she would have him charged under the Mann Act.

Passed in 1910 and named for its author, Illinois Congressman James Robert Mann, the law made it a felony to engage in interstate or foreign commerce transport of "any woman or girl for the purpose of prostitution or debauchery, or for any other immoral purpose." The intention of the law was to prevent "white slavery," not a tryst across the Illinois border into Wisconsin. But the law had teeth. The boxer Jack Johnson had been arrested twice for violations. Future arrests would include Frank Lloyd Wright, Charlie Chaplin, Charles Manson, and Chuck Berry.

Perhaps Guszkowski thought this was the end of it, a détente. They returned to Chicago. After that, Guszkowski got at least one warning not to eat or drink anything that Tillie gave him. His sister, Stella, had quarreled with the woman, but Tillie later gave her candy, perhaps meant to be seen as a peace offering. That candy made Stella "deathly ill." She recovered, lucky not to find herself in the All Saints Cemetery. But Guszkowski didn't learn that lesson. He accepted food and moonshine from Tillie, and a month later, he followed her two husbands to the grave.

When Frank Kupczyk became her third husband, how could he know Tillie would purchase a bargain coffin for him while he was still alive and then celebrate his death with jazz? Through these four men, three of them unwitting husbands, she was perfecting her methods of killing. But Joseph Klimek, the man who would be her last husband, would also be her undoing.

Joseph Klimek knew Frank Kupczyk from the neighborhood. The day he and some friends called on Frank as he lay dying, he met Frank's soon-to-be widow, probably still working on her funeral outfit. Joseph's first marriage had been a long and happy one, but his wife had been dead for some time. The papers later described him as a "lonely, hard working, susceptible widower," who was "slow of thought, passive of temper, and inadequate of action."

When Joseph showed up at Frank's funeral, he must have seemed an ideal candidate to Tillie. He had a steady job and a good nature. He was fifty-one. She was forty-five. The friends who had introduced them urged Joseph to "settle down."

Joseph said later that he had "married Tillie for a home." He'd heard tell of her good cooking, and she "gave every evidence of being an old-fashioned wife."

After they married, Tillie demonstrated her devotion by "burning up all the photographs of her previous husbands and man friends." She tore up her love letters and put Joseph's picture on the mantel in their apartment. He believed they were happy. They went to the movies occasionally. According to Joseph, she never raised her voice to him and they never argued. Later, he admitted that "she gadded around a lot in the day time" and he "didn't know where she went, but she was always there to get my supper. She was never late." He loved her food and was proud that she "crocheted fine bedspreads."

One day, though, Joseph overheard Tillie talking about him to her son. "If anything is wrong," he told her, "I'll get out of the house." But she "preferred to have him remain, on neutral good terms, and she presided over his weekly wage." And besides, men didn't leave Tillie. Not without consequences.

Joseph's easygoing nature may have been what spared him for so long. Every Saturday, he brought his $26/week salary home. Tillie kept it and gave him $1 each morning before work. When he got sick, Tillie claimed that his drinking had made him ill, that he spent $6 a day on whiskey. Joseph was incredulous, pointing to his meager allowance: "That was my money, and you can't buy much hooch with that." He even believed that his reputation as a "tightwad" was what attracted Tillie to him.

After a year of marriage, she pushed him to take out a life insurance policy. Then she went to talk to her cousin Nellie. Allegedly, Tillie asked her cousin for advice on "the trouble she was having with her husband." Nellie advised her to get a divorce, but Tillie said, "No, I will get rid of him some other way." At that, Nellie purportedly "went to the cupboard and gave her dissatisfied cousin a good portion of 'Rough on Rats,'" a poison that would, according to its ads, "clear out rats, mice, roaches, ants, bedbugs, skunks, chipmunks, and gophers." It was 90 percent arsenic. Rough on Rats' slogan "Don't Die in the House" apparently didn't apply to husbands.

"Rough on Rats" advertisement, 1901.

Later, Assistant State's Attorney Edward J. Lyons would testify that Tillie confessed to this conversation while in custody and that Nellie corroborated her story. When the trial came around, both women denied it. During the investigation and trial, though, Nellie's own poisoning expertise would come out. Arsenic, and Rough on Rats in particular, it seemed, sat right alongside all the other well-used housekeeping products in the women's homes. The extent of their poisoning would shock Chicagoans to their bones.

Between 1875 and 1920, Chicago saw a four-fold increase in the number of homicides committed by women; the proportion of female murderers to male grew by nearly one-third. During this time, more than twice as many Chicagoans "died at the hands of local women as died from labor violence in the city renowned for its bloody strikes." Relatives counted for nearly 80 percent of those victims, compared to only 27 percent of the victims of male killers. Husbands, not surprisingly, made up the majority of victims. Based on police records, newspaper accounts of homicides, coroners' reports, prison records, court documents, and health department records, one study estimated that over a hundred women killed their husbands during this forty-five year stretch in Chicago, that number spiking between 1910 and 1920. And this doesn't take into account the women who were never suspected or arrested.

The late nineteenth century and early twentieth century saw a spate of poisonings, in particular. A *Chicago Tribune* article in 1911 called poisoning the "newest murder mania" that the "world must combat," and suggested that there was "no more grisly shadow ... no deeper dread" than the worry of food and drink being poisoned by loved ones." Along with strychnine and mercury, arsenic was a common and effective toxin. The French called it *poudre de succession*, inheritance powder.

The wry French euphemism belies the nightmare of dying by arsenic poisoning. Victims vomit and excrete blood and suffer from excruciating abdominal pain. It results in encephalopathy—permanent brain damage that presents as confusion, delirium, psychosis, or coma. The limbs become stiff, numb, and unusable. Victims of arsenic poisoning often wish for death before they're done.

In order to convict someone of murder by poisoning, it wasn't enough to confirm that poisoning had occurred (symptoms resembled other potentially fatal conditions including complications from influenza); criminal intent needed to be proven. During Tillie's trial, the prosecution had to verify that arsenic wasn't a component of the embalming fluid or in high concentrations in the grave soil, as it often was. Arsenic could be an excellent method to avoid detection and collect insurance money.

The fear of women poisoners was palpable in the statements by the prosecution and judge during Tillie's trial. Assistant State's Attorney William F. McLaughlin asked for the death penalty. "This defendant is like a good many other women in this town. She thinks she can get away with it. There are a lot of women, gentlemen, who are awaiting your verdict on this case. I feel that the death penalty should be inflicted, and I mean it." He was looking for a deterrent that would "put a pausing hand on the hands of those fiends who, in the future, may think of sprinkling poison on their husband's food." Judge Marcus Kavanaugh added, "I venture to say there are more husbands poisoned in this community than the police or authorities realize."

With several decades of fighting for women's suffrage and the 1920 signing into law of the Nineteenth Amendment giving them the right to vote, the perception of women's role in society was changing. And not to everyone's comfort. How to reconcile the sacrosanct images of motherhood and moral housewifery with the new voting woman? It would be all too easy to associate their increasing freedom and enfranchisement with loose morals, carnality, and even criminality. Though the vote didn't materially change their circumstances, women unleashed were a threat in the minds of many men.

Still, the very real rising numbers of female murderers, and poisoners in particular, drove Assistant State's Attorney McLaughlin and Judge Kavanaugh's anxiety. Tillie and Nellie were far from the only women who attempted, succeeded, and were caught for murder during the Jazz Age. Most of these suspected female killers were found not guilty. A novel path to acquittal was being trailblazed; a "new unwritten law gave a woman the right to use lethal force in resisting an abusive husband," and "Chicago husband killers explicitly invoked the new unwritten law." This "legal strategy enraged local prosecutors." In the previous few years, twenty-eight women were acquitted of murder in Chicago; only four were found guilty. The men in the legal system also believed that the attractiveness of the defendant influenced juries, still all men and still susceptible to their own notions of femininity and the propriety of imprisoning or executing women.

Bias aside, McLaughlin and Kavanaugh were right to be worried. Tillie and her cousin would succeed in generating a body count to rival any of the Jazz Age killers. And Tillie was bent on adding her latest husband, Joseph Klimek, to the list.

5

Dogs were dying in the neighborhood. In short order, their owners would follow—people who had quarreled with or otherwise crossed Tillie. If anyone in the years before Tillie married Joseph Klimek noticed the pattern and wondered to each other about the strange plague that was taking down dog and human alike, nobody said anything to the authorities.

Then Joseph's two dogs died after eating table scraps. Tillie's table scraps. Joseph wasn't feeling at all well himself. No sooner had he passed the medical examination to qualify for the life insurance policies Tillie convinced him to buy than he got violently ill. And Tillie's predictions began. As Joseph suffered and struggled to walk, Tillie assured him "you are pretty near dead now," and "didn't I tell you, you aren't going to live long?" If Joseph's brother John hadn't gotten involved, coffin shopping and dancing to jazz might have ensued. But Joseph's worsening condition worried John. Remembering the death of the dogs, he called in a doctor over Tillie's objections.

After two visits, Dr. Peter T. Burns diagnosed Joseph with "arsenical poisoning." He later testified, "He had all the symptoms. He had a garlic breath and walked with great stiffness." Tillie, the doctor claimed, had a "merry twinkle in her eyes," when he voiced his conclusions. He immediately had Joseph taken to the hospital, maybe as much to get him out of Tillie's clutches as to treat the poisoning.

After years of dispatching husbands and neighbors, Tillie's exploits finally drew the attention of the authorities. Tests performed at the hospital gave no doubt about the cause of Joseph's paralysis and other symptoms. There was "free arsenic" in his body. Doctors feared that he would be "permanently crippled from the effects of the poison." They called in the police.

Lieutenant Willard K. Malone took Tillie into custody on October 26, 1922. Malone's persistent investigation would uncover a "poison ring" that had been killing for years. At the time, she was only charged with attempting to kill Joseph, who was still recuperating in the hospital from his close call. Responsible not only for arresting her, but for developing the case against her, even Malone found himself in Tillie's crosshairs. Riding in "the wagon," Tillie wagged her finger at him and said, "The next one I want to cook a dinner for is you. You made all my trouble."

Photograph of Tillie Klimek, 1922.

Malone also arrested her son from her first marriage, Joseph Mitkiewicz Jr. Of three, he was her only surviving child and had lived with Tillie through every marriage and every death. He worked at an electrotyping plant. The electrotype process, used in the nineteenth and early twentieth centuries to create reproductions of engraved metal plates in printing and sculptures in art, used one chemical in particular in large quantities: arsenic. Rough on Rats, then, wasn't Tillie's only potential source of the poison. Searching the Klimek home, Malone found a bottle of arsenic, but Mitkiewicz claimed it belonged to a former boarder, a nurse. That first day Tillie was in custody, she turned police attention away from her son and on to her cousin Nellie Koulik. Mitkiewicz was released, uncharged. It was Nellie, as Tillie told Assistant State's Attorney Lyons, who gave her the "white powder" she sprinkled on her husband's food. Tillie was tired, she said, of "the way he fooled around with other women."

Still, Joseph was her husband, and she wanted to visit him at West Side Hospital. Perhaps Lieutenant Malone and Assistant State's Attorney Lyons thought an encounter between victim and perpetrator would yield further insight into the case. Maybe Tillie would slip up, or the sight of her suffering husband would prompt further confession, if not contrition. So, with the police on one arm and the court on the other, Tillie visited Joseph.

She kissed her husband when she entered his room. Joseph in his hospital bed wasn't too weak to rail at her for trying to kill him. Tillie just said, "I don't know. Don't bother me anymore." But Joseph would be heard.

> She heard him denounce her, heard him plan to divorce her, heard him thank God that he had found her out. And when he had finished, she went over to the bed, and without a trace of anger, without a tear, a shiver, without a plea for mercy or a denial of guilt, remarked cooly, as she kissed him: "Jo, I don't think they're treating you right here. You'd better come home with me."

Joseph said he'd "prosecute her." Then he asked the nurse for a glass of water.

Tillie told her, "If he makes any trouble for you take a two by four board and hit him over the head with it."

Later, Joseph would tell the press that he believed that he had been the "victim of a plot." "Still weak from the effects of the poison," he told reporters "in a timid, honest, childish, and at times, amused way, of his wife's transition from a home loving Penelope to a husband killing Lucretia Borgia."

After Tillie's implication of her cousin Nellie in the crime, Malone began to take seriously the possibility of a deliberate plot. Nellie Koulik was arrested at the box factory where she worked. Initially, she was only charged as an accessory to Joseph's attempted murder. But then, the police received an anonymous letter about Nellie and her late husband. "Have the body of Mr. Sturmer, who died some years back, exhumed and you will see that he was poisoned," it read.

T he more Malone and his team of investigators dug, the more they found. When the anonymous letter came, he widened the scope of the investigation. Though the official cause of Nellie Koulik's first husband's death was pneumonia, it turned out there had been neighborhood gossip at the time that he died of poisoning. Neighbors and family members began to come out of the woodwork with poisoning claims against the two women.

Both were held at West Chicago Avenue police station. Tillie greeted all interviewers "defiantly." Her cousin Nellie was in a "better mood." She "chatted gayly with jailers and when brought into a room to meet her husband, she made him the target of good-natured gibes." Nellie was particular about her appearance in photographs, insisting that the photographer wait until she "slicked her hair." Tillie hid her face and refused to pose.

Coroner Peter Hoffman started an inquiry and within days had received permission from relatives to exhume suspected victims' bodies. The first to be dug up was Frank Kupczyk, the husband Tillie had bought a bargain coffin for. Meanwhile, Malone, along with Detective Sergeants Balata and Swenson, the other investigating officers, canvassed the neighborhoods where the cousins had lived, looking for more information on other possible poisonings.

They found it. And it wasn't limited to Tillie and Nellie.

Cornelia Kozlowski and her daughter Martha Mitky, also cousins of Tillie, were implicated in a "poison plot." Kozlowski had urged her son-in-law, Nick Mitky, to get insurance, and when he failed to pay the premiums, she took over paying for the $1,000 policy. When Nick visited Tillie shortly after, she gave him a drink of "moonshine," and he hadn't "felt well since." After the arrests of Tillie and Nellie, Mitky went to the police, telling them that he "had pains in his legs." Poison was found at the Mitky house and his wife and mother-in-law were arrested. The possibility of "an arsenic murder trust" would have played right into the fears of the men in Chicago's criminal justice system. Especially when the results of the exhumations started coming in.

The chemical analysis of Frank Kupszyk's body that found arsenic, "enough to kill four men," led Coroner Hoffman to request the exhumation of Tillie's first husband, Joseph Mitkiewicz, and based on the anonymous letter, Wojicik Sturmer, Nellie's first husband. Then they dug up John Ruszkakski, Tillie's second husband.

Joseph Mitkiewicz's organs were found to contain 11.2 milligrams of arsenic more than the amount that killed Frank. John Ruszkakski had 13.8 milligrams in him. The coroner's chemist found "enough arsenic in the organs to kill several persons" in Wojcik Sturmer. While investigating the death of Ruszkakski, police learned of the death of Guszkowski, the man wise enough not to marry Tillie, but not wise enough to avoid eating her food.

Several of Tillie's relatives came forward. Her cousin Harry Suida called the state's attorney's office about the "mysterious death" of his sister, Rose Chudzinski. Rose and Tillie had quarreled, but Rose still accepted an invitation to dinner at Tillie's house. Then she died. Cousin Elizabeth Wyieckowski told of the "mysterious deaths of two sisters and a brother after eating at Tillie's." Both Suida & Wyieckowski asked for the exhumation of their relatives to test them for poison. Tillie and her cousin Francis Zakrzewski lived together for a time and allegedly quarreled. Shortly after, Francis' three children died. Helen was fifteen, Stanley was sixteen, and Stella was twenty-three.

The accusations kept coming. The sister-in-law of Tillie's third husband, Frank, said she got sick after eating at Tillie's and was still under the care of a doctor. Rose Splitt and Guszkowski's sister, Stella, both came forward to tell the police about the poisoned candy that Tillie gave them. Splitt believed that Tillie was jealous because she'd been talking with Joseph Klimek, and Stella had argued with Tillie. Slights that, in Tillie's world, carried potentially fatal consequences.

Cousin Nellie faced her own raft of accusations. Her own daughter came forward, claiming there had been "friction" between Nellie and her when her small daughter, Dorothy, came down with a cold. Nellie insisted her two-year-old granddaughter be brought to her for care. The baby's face swelled up and her condition became dangerous. She died at Nellie's home. With Nellie's arrest, the parents insisted that their baby's body be exhumed.

Then the investigators started asking questions about Nellie's own kids. She had given birth to sixteen children—six were dead. Her son John took ill around the time of Wojcik Sturmer's death and believed he was poisoned by his mother. His fifteen-year-old sister, Lillian Sturmer, also told police that she "was made deathly sick by food" her mother fed her. She continued to "suffer from heart trouble." She and John would help the prosecution build the case against Nellie.

The authorities opened up the graves in St. Adalbert's Cemetery of Nellie's granddaughter, Dorothy, and two of Nellie's children, as well. She was accused of killing her seven-month-old twins "because their crying annoyed her." There were also rumors that the twins, Sophie and Benjamin, were actually the children of a man who was a roomer at her house when Nellie was married to Wojcik Sturmer.

Malone, suspecting the women of even more murders, called this extensive list of victims "incomplete." The women's denials of their early confessions notwithstanding, exhumed bodies full of arsenic don't lie. Tillie maintained she was a "victim of a back fence, doorstep, 'kaffeklatch' plot," insisting that it was all neighborhood gossip, "recollected in revenge," and that she was a "good housekeeper."

Her denials became more vehement: "I didn't rob nobody; I didn't shoot nobody; I didn't kill nobody. I didn't! Everybody pick on me. Everybody makes eyes at me like they going to eat me. Why do they make eyes at me like that? I tell the truth."

But of the eleven of Tillie's relatives exhumed, poison was found in seven of them. Soon, a judge and jury would hear Tillie's claims of innocence and weigh them against all that arsenic. If the prosecutor had his way, it would "mean death at gallows."

Assistant State's Attorney William F. McLaughlin called it the "most astounding wholesale poisoning plot ever uncovered." By the time the two women were arraigned, they would be suspected of killing over twenty men, women, and children. Rumors whispered of even more men "who mysteriously dropped from sight." The authorities made inquiries into "matrimonial agencies and undertaking establishments" to find all possible victims. At the arraignment, the judge even gave the police another ten days to investigate and to continue the chemical analysis of the exhumed bodies. Lieutenant Malone's "incomplete list" was getting longer all the time.

Photograph of Lieutenant Malone, Assistant State's Attorney Peden, and Assistant State's Attorney McLaughlin.

Though the personal stories of the victims were not covered by the newspapers, these were family members, friends, people bound by the ties of community, tradition, and homeland. All shared the immigrant experience—its labors, its promise, its desperations. They worked in the factories and the stockyards. And they were raising their children to be a new thing: Polish Americans. These were Tillie and Nellie's people. Their histories might be lost, but their deaths by poisoning were nothing if not personal.

With the number of likely victims piling up, the state nonetheless went about trying the women's cases methodically. Tillie Klimek was charged only with the murder of Frank Kupczyk, and Nellie Koulik for the murder of her first husband, Wojcik Stermer. Trials for the attempted murder of Joseph Klimek and all the other poisonings would depend on the outcome of the first case. If they couldn't get them on one crime, they had others to charge them with waiting in the wings.

Newspapers often lumped the women together, describing them in physically unflattering terms. The fact that they were not only from the same Polish ghetto, but blood relations supporting each other in the same criminal activity would make it tempting to see them as two Polish poisoner peasants in a pod. The press delighted in calling them the "Lady Bluebeards."

In many ways, though, they were a study in contrasts, and one reporter saw this. Genevieve Forbes of the *Chicago Daily Tribune* would provide a vivid account of the women, the investigation, and the trials. She was able to get access to neighbors, family members, and the defendants themselves and paint a detailed picture of the case. When she visited them in jail, she summed them up by writing that Nellie's "intonation, her gesture, is humble, the attitude of a peasant, where Mrs. Klimek is the patrician, daring herself to ask a favor, or to be feminine." She observed that Nellie "ate her food with a relish," while Tillie "was disdainful of everything." She attributed to Tillie "the hardness of an opportunist in the habit of getting what she wants, the indifferent superiority of a master, the cunning zeal of a creator, the sneer of a cynic, and the detachment of a philosopher as she sits in her cell and baffles all who question her."

When the trial day finally came, the "Lady Bluebeards" sat in the courtroom "stoically, and with no show of emotion." Wearing a simple black dress and the "rigid brimmed sailor hat" that she made at Frank's bedside and wore to his funeral, Tillie tapped the "sensible square toe of her soft black shoe up and down with monotonous precision."

According to Forbes, they were "without guile or the aid of hairdresser, manicure, modiste, or diary. They carry no vanity box, rouge or lipstick." In a different article, Forbes wrote that Tillie has "a greasy complexion and a lumpy figure, growls instead of murmurs, and knows a crochet needle better than a lipstick."

Going by the *Chicago Tribune's* later examination of the cases of women murderers at the time, Tillie's looks were a strike against her. "A woman still can commit murder in Cook County and stand a better than even chance of escaping punishment," the reporter claimed, "especially if she is young and attractive." Tillie was neither.

Forbes wrote that "no sable wrap envelopes slim, white shoulders. A dark red sweater stretches over a form that echoes a comely young figure now gone. No smart frock, but a calico work dress, neat, serviceable, efficient." As Assistant State's Attorney McLaughlin put it, of the four women actually convicted of murder during this period, one was "judged insane," one was "more than middle-aged," and the other two were termed "no beauties." In one case, the prosecutors said, "It is just the same old story. It is almost impossible to convict a woman for killing her husband." In another, the prosecutors realized that "their greatest difficulty in securing a conviction was not the evidence, but the attractiveness of the defendant."

Cases like that of Cora Orthwein, a "pretty divorcée," who killed her married lover in March of 1921, seemed to bear this out. There was little doubt that Orthwein shot Herbert Ziegler, and ample evidence to suggest both jealousy over his attention to other women and rage at his apparent intent to break off their affair. The jury deliberations lasted an hour and came back with an acquittal. The state's attorney in the case said, "You can't convict a pretty woman."

Tillie's peasant looks notwithstanding, all this was undoubtedly in prosecutor McLaughlin's mind when he "sought to show that women were generally treated more leniently than men charged with similar crimes, and specifically in cases of spousal murder." He asked every prospective juror the same question: "You would punish a woman as severely as you would a man, if she were guilty, wouldn't you?"

Tillie was "alone, deserted by relatives, scorned by friends, repudiated by her husband," who was still desperately ill in the hospital. But two people believed unwaveringly in her innocence: her seventy-one-year-old mother and seventy-three-year-old father. Called "two timid peasants," neither spoke English. Forbes wrote that "they have never studied criminal law, nor psychology, nor ethics. They are too primitive to disguise their feelings ... over and over they repeat their statement, in hysteric Polish syllables, that Tillie is innocent."

Mrs. Gburek was "frail, bent, and faded, a fragment from the old world peasantry." Her quasi-paralyzed husband Forbes described as a "white haired, dumb, nonresistant silhouette from the old country" slumping at the kitchen table.

Whether or not her parents' humble presence and staunch support for their daughter would help her case still remained to be seen, but Tillie's genetics were very much on the minds of the authorities. In addition to the debates about leniency toward "lady killers," conversations on biological inheritance and whether these murders could have been prevented were also bubbling to the surface in Tillie's trial. The "science" of eugenics was being debated actively in the justice system of the 1920s, as was a mysterious new diagnosis —a diagnosis of particular relevance for those suspected of heinous crimes.

8

A dolf Hitler would soon become the infamous and terrifying face of eugenics in 1930s Germany, but "the science of better breeding to improve the human race" found popularity decades before, in nineteenth-century England. Starting in 1880, Francis Galton, a cousin of Charles Darwin, "launched a movement to improve the human race, or at least halt its perceived decline, through selective breeding." In eugenics, Galton saw science with a moral imperative. Its appeal to the elite classes grew with the decades until the fascists in Germany adopted it as a rallying cry for the struggling and resentful people of that already war-battered country.

Dr. Harry Campbell, a well-known physician and eugenicist in London at the turn of the century, defined the "object of eugenics as the promotion of the welfare of the human race by encouraging biologically suitable and discouraging biologically unsuitable matings." He called it the "science of man breeding."

And in 1913, a *British Medical Journal* article proclaimed the "importance of human stock-breeding"; the subject was included in an annual meeting of the British Medical Association. The article claimed that "even schoolgirls of 16 are familiar with the question . . . and freely discuss its practical application." The author went on to lament that "under existing social conditions, it was vain to hope for any great or general improvement," but that "if a fraction of the care exercised in the breeding of horses were used in the propagation of the human species, there might be a hope that the race would be vastly improved." The article made the case that "the segregation of the mentally deficient is justified at once in their own interest and in that of the community," and stopped just short of surgical sterilization in its recommendation of methods to accomplish this.

By the 1920s, the eugenics question had been picked up by celebrity thinkers—famous minds embraced it and famous minds abhorred it, but it couldn't be ignored. George Bernard Shaw, the Irish playwright, critic, and author of *Man and Superman* and *Pygmalion,* was a proponent, believing that "nothing but a eugenic religion could save civilization." And Bertrand Russell advocated for it from the perspective of an academic mathematician. H.G. Wells, the author of *The War of the Worlds*, *The Invisible Man*, and *The Island of Doctor Moreau*, though, was a vocal opponent, objecting to Galton's suggestion that "bishops' sons should be encouraged to breed while those of criminals should not."

It was Galton's sentiment that the presiding judge in Nellie's case had firmly in mind when he said, "if we had had a fieldworker, a eugenics expert, to check up on the history of this whole family at the time one moron was discovered, then the police might have been warned to watch this woman and so might possibly have prevented these crimes." Driven by the Koulik case, he intended to "apply to the Carnegie Institute for such a worker and then, we find one case we can seek out and locate the nest."

Both women were evaluated by Dr. William J. Hickson, head of the "psychopathic laboratory" engaged by the municipal court. He concluded that they were "subnormal mentally" and neither had "an intellect higher than that of an 11 year old child." It's unclear what criteria Hickson used for his testing, and whether he took into account their minimal education or that English was their second language.

Hickson had examined one of Nellie's sons years earlier when the boy had appeared before the juvenile court. Hickson found him to "be of feeble mind." The boy was sent to a reformatory. Another of Nellie's sons ended up in juvenile court three times and was currently out on probation from that same reformatory, where he served time for robbery with a gun. On top of the dubious framework of his testing, Hickson likely factored the criminal activity of Nellie's sons into his report.

He concluded that both women suffered from "dementia praecox." Just twenty years earlier, this new medical diagnosis "arrived in the United States with great fanfare." Identified by German psychiatrist Emil Kraepelin in 1893, the disease was described in the new psychology-speak as a "peculiar destruction of the internal connexions of the psychic personality." In 1895, no one in the United States had a diagnosis of dementia praecox. "Ten years later, thousands of Americans had Kraepelin's disease, and the condition was considered epidemic." The implicit meaning of the diagnosis was "chronic, incurable insanity." The term, generally unfamiliar now, "was perhaps the most discussed disease of the first half of the twentieth century." Dementia praecox was eventually replaced with the "alternative disease label, schizophrenia."

Their genetics picked apart, their intelligence determined to be "subnormal," and their brains diagnosed as diseased, it might follow that verdicts of not guilty by reason of insanity were at least a possibility for the women. But in the end, all the debating of biology didn't meaningfully alter the legal arguments, and in Tillie's case, none of it would help the woman so good at "predicting" the fates of others escape her own.

In her plain black silk dress and the black sailor hat, Tillie watched the proceedings implacably. Early in the trial, she giggled at the prosecution's struggle to pronounce all the Polish names. With the exception of these rare moments, Tillie would seem "unmoved and apparently unshaken."

Genevieve Forbes took her demeanor to mean that she was "bored and confused by the legal phraseology." Another reporter assumed she was "bewildered by the technical references to milligrams, positive results, and anatomical terms."

Photograph of the trial.

McLaughlin called a series of witnesses: "three gravediggers and a lady undertaker," six physicians, a chemist, four nurses, and a trio of insurance agents. These last three got Tillie's attention. She "seemed to be checking the accuracy of the figures as the insurance agents told of the money paid to the widow on the deaths of her first and second husbands, and of the money coming to her on the death of Frank." Neighbors testified to Tillie's prediction of Frank's death and to her cold hearted and cavalier conduct while he suffered.

Assistant State's Attorney Edward J. Lyons testified to the confession Tillie made to him on October 27, and the corroboration by Nellie. He was specific in the details of what the women said. The Rough on Rats, the meat Tillie sprinkled it on and then fed to Joseph while he was in a "semi-intoxicated condition"—details like these, and particularly the animated testimony of the gravedigger who saw Tillie kissing a man while slowly poisoning Frank, made for a raucous courtroom. Judge Kavanaugh "frequently reminded his giggling audience that '[t]his is not theater.'"

Finally called to the stand, Tillie never once wavered in her denial during the three-hour cross-examination. Asked if she was responsible for Frank's death, she answered, "he died by moonshine."

Did she have "any trouble with any of her husbands"?

"I did not," said Tillie. "I loved them. They loved me. They died same as other people. I not responsible for that. I could not help if they wanted to die."

McLaughlin was confident he'd get a conviction and eager to secure the death penalty. The twelve-man jury took only an hour and twenty minutes to decide her fate. When the sentence was read, "Tillie sat so still she made her neighbors wriggle uncomfortably."

Guilty. The jury decided it on their first ballot.

On their second ballot, four of them voted for the death

penalty. On their third and final ballot, they came to a unanimous agreement. But instead of the death penalty that Assistant State's Attorney McLaughlin had pressed so hard for, the judge read that the jury "fixed her punishment at life imprisonment."

When Judge Kavanaugh stopped talking, Tillie "turned her face upwards and smiled." On the way back to her cell, all she said was "it was warm in there."

Kavanaugh denied the defense's motion for a new trial. "I venture to say there are more husbands poisoned in this community than the police or authorities realize."

Sentenced to Joliet penitentiary, Tillie was the first woman in Cook County to be found guilty of murdering her husband. But McLaughlin quickly had another chance to argue that poisoners, male or female, deserved to die. The jury would shortly reconvene to decide if Nellie Koulik would share her cousin's fate or maybe something much worse.

Nellie on the stand was a different creature altogether from her strident cousin. "Every line in her face and figure and voice sagged." On the "charges of murder and assault to murder," Prosecutor McLaughlin hoped to succeed—from conviction to capital punishment—with the second case, where the first came up short.

Nellie's attorneys described her as "a plain, hard working woman." The prosecution called her a "faithless wife," who "chose the cowardly poison route." They argued that Nellie's motive was both her liking for Albert Koulik, who would become her husband after the death of Wójcik Sturmer, and the insurance money she would receive when Sturmer died.

A neighbor, Joseph Terek, testified that he had witnessed "twilight petting parties" on the back porch of the house Nellie lived in with Wójcik Sturmer, her first husband. It wasn't Sturmer he saw Nellie embracing, though; it was her boarder, Albert Koulik. "And that was not all I saw," Terek claimed. The courtroom loved it. Judge Kavanaugh had to silence their laughter. The *Chicago Tribune* called Terek's racy testimony about the "petting parties" the highlight of the day's proceedings.

Matters sobered up when three of Nellie's sons and her daughter took the witness stand against her. They described the arguments between their parents and Nellie's fights with one of her sons. They testified that Nellie cooked and served "all the meals eaten by Sturmer before his death."

But her children also seemed reluctant to testify against her, despite a couple of them having been poison victims themselves. When the court adjourned, "they moved forward and surrounded their mother. They all cried." Except for one: her son John.

The jury took twenty-two hours and five ballots before they were done. First, it was seven to five for acquittal, then ten to two, and there it remained. The jury "had been unable to decide whether or not the 'unbeautiful' mother of twelve children had given arsenic to her first husband."

"Is there any chance of you men coming to an agreement?" Judge Kavanaugh asked the foreman.

"We cannot agree, your honor. We stand the same now as we did this morning ... The stumbling point," the foreman declared, "was a question of fact, not law."

Two of them simply could not vote to acquit the "'mid-channel' vamp." By default, Nellie Koulik was found not guilty of murdering her first husband anyway.

The forty-eight-year-old woman, who looked sixty, "burst into tears." Her mood veered promptly into bitterness and fury, though, as she turned on her eldest son.

"It all come about," she shrieked, "because that fella, John, he told that on me. He told it in a joke, just a joke, and the big men, they believe me." When John tried to explain, Nellie yelled at him in Polish. The other children "glowered at him" and he "rushed out of the room." Nellie shouted the same Polish phrases after him, louder and louder.

Wasting no time, McLaughlin pressed charges for "assault with intent to murder Joseph Klimek," and Nellie was sent back to jail to await trial on the second charge. By the time the second trial started, Joseph Klimek had been discharged from the hospital where he'd fought for ten months against death by arsenic. This time, however, the jury returned a verdict of not guilty on the first ballot. Whatever the differences between Nellie and her cousin Tillie—whether in demeanor or appearance—they apparently made all the difference in the world.

"Ma" Koulik, "with the watery blue eyes, the figureless figure, and the same drab clothes of a year ago, freed from worries of law, turned her attention to the pleasures of life." Reporters tried to interview her. "Them newspaper people," she said, "I don't want I should be bothered with them. Get a lawyer man to throw them out."

Somebody asked her how she was treated in jail. After a long pause, she answered, "My God, they were swell," and once again began to cry. Why she was never tried for the killings of her granddaughter and other family members is unknown. She simply claimed the "few belongings" she had given up when she was arrested and, before getting into a cab with three of her sons, "Ma" Koulik thanked the jailors and guards for their "kindness to her."

Albert Koulik, Nellie's husband, wasn't rejoicing at her release. He was filing for divorce. Those nights on Wójcik Sturmer's porch, fooling around with the man's wife, now his wife, must have seemed like a dream. A dream that could easily have been one box of Rough on Rats away from turning into a nightmare for him. "I wouldn't live with that woman another hour," he said.

Tillie's imprisonment and Nellie's acquittal would signal an end to years of their collaborative killing. Together, the women had taken innumerable neighbors and family members violently to the grave. Some with a jazz send off.

Epilogue

Thirteen years was all Tillie Klimek would serve of her life sentence for the murder of Frank Kupczyk. In 1936, at the age of 64, she died of heart disease. A quicker and far less painful end than the one she gave her victims. Nellie disappeared from the public record. Just as the Spanish flu claimed its dead and moved on, the epidemic of female poisoners in the United States reached a nadir and receded from the cultural consciousness to be replaced with other murder manias.

But questions remain. Of the poison ring that Lieutenant Malone uncovered, why did Tillie Klimek alone serve time? With such a methodical prosecution, and evidence of foul play extending beyond the murder of Nellie Koulik's first husband, why did McLaughlin leave off trying to convict Nellie of other poisonings after she was acquitted a second time? And what of Tillie's other cousins, Cornelia Kozlowski and her daughter Martha Mitky, who were arrested and then released? What in the culture or biology of this family produced at least two, maybe four killers? If Malone's "incomplete list" truly pointed to dozens of victims at the hands of these women, how could a city as hungry for law and order as Chicago let it go at a single conviction?

Some answers may lie at the crossroads of gender and the

legal system. William McLaughlin was interested in convictions, not a long chain of trials that ended in acquittals. The evidence against Kozlowski and Mitky may have been too circumstantial to proceed. But even ironclad evidence sometimes wasn't enough. As McLaughlin was well aware, he was up against society's perceptions of women. A frail woman, an attractive woman, even an emotional mother, like Nellie Koulik, played to male jurors' sympathies and notions of femininity. A tug of war was afoot between the fear of female poisoners and the prevailing image of women that prevented their punishment.

That tug-of-war played out throughout the Jazz Age. Poisoner Anna Tomaskiewicz killed as many as four husbands in Massachusetts. Her home was called a "murder factory," but the jury still found her not guilty by reason of insanity. In Texas, Dessie Keyes got away with killing a man, a woman, and a baby despite a signed confession. Edith Murray is believed to have killed three husbands and two children in Cleveland but was never prosecuted. And these are just a handful of the cases in the first years of the 1920s.

McLaughlin may have simply decided the odds were not in his favor, and there were other more likely convictions to be made with the rise of the Chicago mob. For once, male bias worked in women's favor. The irony is, of course, that the women were murderers.

The Klimek and Koulik cases weren't the last time McLaughlin would face this stumbling block to conviction. In 1924, he was on the prosecution team that sought the death penalty for Beulah Annan, a strikingly beautiful married woman who'd murdered her lover right in the bedroom she shared with her husband. Annan and Belva Gaertner, another "murderess" in Cook County Prison, were so aware of how their looks played to the press, the public, and the jury, that they started a jailhouse "fashion school" for female criminals.

No juryman in Jazz Age Chicago could resist the likes of Annan's giant blue eyes, flowing red hair, and pouty lips. McLaughlin and his team once again failed to bring female murderers to justice.

Annan and Gaertner's infamy would grow with the years and the publishing of a play based on their exploits, written by Maureen Watkins, the woman who covered the trial for the *Chicago Tribune*. *Chicago* would go on to become one of the most popular musicals of the twentieth century.

Tillie Klimek and Nellie Koulik killed many more people than Annan and Gaertner and couldn't rely on their looks to avoid punishment. That Koulik was acquitted and Klimek avoided the worst punishment after so many horrific crimes speak to the fact that men's squeamishness at punishing female criminals ran deeper than mere attractiveness.

The country would continue to reckon with the changing role of women, their increased property rights, ability to dissolve marriages, and claims to maintain custody of their children. Fear of women would endure, manifesting in other ways. But, in Chicago, the rising number of homicides committed by women in the early twentieth century would level off, and the citizens of "Little Warsaw" could rest a little easier knowing that at least one poisoner could no longer season their dinners.

A Word From C.J. March

Thank you for reading *Poison Widow*. If you have thoughts on this book or suggestions for other true crime accounts, please let us know at cjmarch@deadtruecrime.com. We love hearing from readers. You're why we write.

Sign up for our mailing list to learn about new Dead True Crime books and to read and listen to a free, exclusive story: www.deadtruecrime.com/ebook.

If you're interested in reading more Tillie Klimek, check out the bibliography at the end of the book.

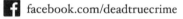 facebook.com/deadtruecrime

 twitter.com/deadtruecrime

Other Dead True Crime Books

Sacrificial Axe
Voodoo Cult Slayings in the Deep South

The "Axe-man" came in the night. No one heard him come. No locks could keep him out. In the morning, whole families lay slaughtered in their beds, a riot of blood corrupting the room. Town by town, terror gripped the black communities of Louisiana and East Texas, as men, women, and children fell to the killer's ax. The police were powerless to stop it. Was it simply a homicidal maniac on the loose, or was a deeper evil afoot? Could one person perpetrate over forty atrocities? Was the serial killer even a man? People whispered voodoo, and white newspapers in the Jim Crow era South fanned the hysteria. As the police slowly unraveled the mystery, they were stunned by the bizarre truth of the "Axe-man."

Get Sacrificial Axe

Ghoul of Grays Harbor: Murder and Mayhem in the Pacific Northwest

Sailors trusted him with their money and their lives. That was a mistake. The lucky ones woke up with headaches in the holds of ships headed to China. The others never took another breath.

Billy Gohl robbed, 'shanghaied,' and killed sailors across the Pacific Northwest. Grays Harbor in Aberdeen, Washington was so full of bodies that newspapers dubbed it a 'floaters fleet.' His trapdoor of death was famous. In his time, Gohl murdered over 100 people, making him one of the most prolific serial killers in American history.

Get Ghoul of Grays Harbor

Murderer's Gulch
Carnage in the Catskills

Don't turn your back on her. Don't even blink. She may be crazy, but Lizzie Halliday is strong, she moves fast, and she's a stone cold killer. When famed journalist Nellie Bly interviews the woman the New York Times called "The Worst Woman on Earth," she has no idea how easy it would be for Lizzie Halliday to make Bly her next victim. In the peaceful Catskills in upstate New York, Halliday dispatches husbands, neighbors and peddlers by fire, poisoning and gunshot. The bloody death count at the Halliday farm earns it the name, "Murderer's Gulch." But even after she's arrested and committed to an insane asylum, Lizzie Halliday will kill again.

Get Murderer's Gulch

Killer Genius

The Bizarre Case of the Homicidal Scholar

He's a doctor whose patients have a way of dying; a lawyer, who uses his skills to squirm out of criminal convictions. He's a scholar, but other scholars have no idea what he's talking about. He's a family man, but one day, his wife and baby disappear forever. Only two things are clear: Edward Rulloff is a mystery, and everywhere he goes, death and destruction follow. While the criminal justice system has its hands full trying to keep and convict Edward Rulloff, the world will argue whether he's a genius, a scam artist or a madman. Even Mark Twain has an opinion.

Get Killer Genius

Coming Soon

Exit Row
Mass Murder in the Canadian Sky

A clear day. An experienced pilot. A routine flight. An obsessive love-triangle. What could go wrong? When a mysterious package follows J. Albert Guay's wife on board Flight 108, calamity is just a few ticks of the clock away. How far will a man go for his adulterous passion?

Cannibal Cowboy
Murder and Man-Eating on the American Frontier

Gold Rush and gunfights, scalping and saloons, the Old West had a reputation to uphold. But even the rough and tumble frontier wasn't ready for the likes of the Kentucky Cannibal. Mountain man and gunfighter Boone Helm would do anything to survive, right down to eating his enemies. Or his friends.

Blood Trade
Slaughter on the Underground Railroad

Nothing could be worse than slavery. Unless it was Patty Cannon hunting you down. A gang of thugs at her command, the woman infamous for her blood-thirst and brutality murdered free blacks and fugitive slaves alike for decades. Working her illegal slave trade in what became known as the Reverse Underground Railroad, Cannon's grisly tactics still have the power to chill centuries later.

About the Author

C.J. March is the alter ego of three true crime enthusiasts who wanted to write the kind of juicy noir histories they like to read. Between them they have: 2 MFAs, 3 arrests, 4 folk albums, 73 years of therapy, 1 stint working for "the artist formerly known as" which ended in a shoving match, 40 years of writing, 30 years of design, 3 dogs, and 1 overnight in a cell with a murderer.

Bibliography

"3 Sons, Daughter Testify Against 'Poison Cousin.'"
Chicago Daily Tribune, April 10, 1923.

"4 More Deaths Cast Shadow On 'Poison Woman.'"
Chicago Daily Tribune, November 7, 1922.

Adler, Jeffrey S. "I Loved Joe, But I had to Shoot Him:
Homicide by Women in Turn-of-the-Century
Chicago." *Journal of Criminal Law and Criminology*
92, nos. 3–4 (Spring-Summer 2002): 867–898.

"Alleged Poison Plot Victims." *Buffalo Times*, February
25, 1923.

"Almost All Arsenic." *New York Times*, May 26, 1888.

"Arsenic Cousins Go on Trial with Air of Peasants."
Chicago Daily Tribune, March 7, 1923.

"Bluebeard Tactics Charged." *Los Angeles Times*, March
12, 1923.

Boulter, Michael. "The Rise of Eugenics, 1901–14."
Chap. 7 in *Bloomsbury Scientists: Science and Art in the
Wake of Darwin*. Los Angeles: UCLA Press, 2017.

Burke, Chloe S., and Christopher J. Castaneda. "The
Public and Private History of Eugenics: An
Introduction." *Public Historian* 29, no. 3 (Summer
2007).

"Chicago's 'Little Warsaw'; The Pulse of Poland in
America's Heartland." *Christian Science Monitor*,
February 4, 1982.

"Convict Woman Poisoner." *Los Angeles Times*, March
14, 1923.

Crane, Elaine Forman. *The Poison Plot: A Tale of
Adultery and Murder in Colonial Newport*. Ithaca:
Cornell University Press, 2018.

"Crime Drive is Begun in Chicago." *Journal of the American Institute of Criminal Law and Criminology* 11, no. 4 (February 1921).

"Death Pictured as Mere Routine in Poison Home." *Chicago Daily Tribune*, November 15, 1922.

"Don't Die in the House." *Washington Post*, October 1, 1883.

"Eugenics." *British Medical Journal* 2, no. 2747 (August 23, 1913)

"Extend Poison Case Net." *Los Angeles Times*, November 20, 1922.

"Find Cook County Juries Kind to 'Lady Killers.'" *Chicago Daily Tribune*, July 28, 1935.

"Gave Jazz Requiem to Husband Victim." *Philadelphia Inquirer*, March 9, 1923.

"Grave Digger Tells of Goings on at Klimek's." *Chicago Daily Tribune*, March 10, 1923.

"Guilty is the Klimek Verdict." *Chicago Daily Tribune*, March 14, 1923.

"H.P. Ziegler Killed by Rich Divorcée." *New York Times*, March 2, 1921.

"Hostess at Poison Banquet Gets Life for Her Crimes." *New York Daily News*, July 5, 1925.

"How Mrs. Klimek Jested of Death of Husband Told." *Chicago Daily Tribune*, March 9, 1923.

"'I Never Did,' Ma Koulik's Defense Plea." *Chicago Daily Tribune*, April 12, 1923.

"Indict 2 Women in Poison Cases; Below Normal." *Chicago Daily Tribune*, November 22, 1922.

"Judge Dismisses Koulik Jury; 2 For Conviction." *Chicago Daily Tribune*, April 14, 1923.

"Klimek Poison Charges Ready for Grand Jury." *Chicago Daily Tribune*, November 18, 1922.

"'Lady Bluebeards' Face Poison Trial Stoically." *Washington Post*, March 7, 1923.

"Law of Eugenics. Who Should Marry?" *Argus*. March 6, 1914.

"'Ma' Koulik, Wise in Jail Learning, Goes Back Home." *Chicago Daily Tribune*, November 9, 1923.

"'Mrs. Bluebeards' of Klimek Case and 20 Alleged Victims." *Chicago Daily Tribune*, November 19, 1922.

"Mrs. Cora Orthwein Is at Liberty after Acquittal of Slaying." *Los Angeles Herald*, June 25, 1921.

"Mrs. Klimek Is Formally Held in Poison Death." *Chicago Daily Tribune*, November 11, 1922.

"Mystery Deaths in Poison Case May Reach 20." *Chicago Daily Tribune*, November 14, 1922.

"Nellie Koulik on Trial for Poisoning Husband." *Belvidere Daily Republican* (Belvidere, IL), November 6, 1923.

Perry, Douglas. *The Girls of Murder City: Fame, Lust, and the Beautiful Killers Who Inspired Chicago.* New York: Viking Penguin, 2010.

"Poison Deaths May Total 12; Babes Victims?" *Chicago Daily Tribune*, November 12, 1922.

"Poison Evidence Robs Mrs. Klimek of Indifference." *Chicago Daily Tribune*, March 11, 1923.

"Poison Murders Hard to Solve." *New York Times*, October 14, 1923.

"Poisoning with Dread Diseases: Newest Murder Mania World Must Combat." *Chicago Daily Tribune*, February 12, 1911.

"Police Suspect 2 Mrs. Bluebeards in Klimek Case." *Chicago Daily Tribune*, November 4, 1922.

"Police to Delve Anew for Clews to Poisonings." *Chicago Daily Tribune*, November 16, 1922.

"Polish Immigration to the United States before

World War II: An Overview." *Polish American Studies* 39, no. 1 (Spring 1982).

"Report Koulik Jury Split, 7-5." *Chicago Daily Tribune*, April 13, 1923.

Robertson, George M. Review of *Dementia Praecox and Paraphrenia,* by Emil Kraepelin, *British Medical Journal* 2, no. 3075 (December 6, 1919).

"Rough on Rats." *Chicago Daily Tribune*, October 14, 1882.

"Says She Admits Poisoning." *Washington Post*, October 28, 1922.

"Seize Two in Poison Mystery." *Chicago Daily Tribune*, October 27, 1922.

Shapiro, Andrea. "Unequal before the Law: Men, Women and the Death Penalty," *Journal of Gender, Social Policy & the Law* 8, no.2 (2000).

Staub, Michael E. Review of *American Madness: The Rise and Fall of Dementia Praecox*, by Richard Noll, *American Historical Review* 117, no. 4 (October 2012).

"TELLS..PART..IN..POISON..PLOT." *Los Angeles Times*, November 13, 1922.

"Tillie Klimek Is Strong Witness in Own Defense." *Chicago Daily Tribune*, March 13, 1923.

"Tillie Klimek, 'Poison Widow,' Gets Life Term." *Chicago Daily Tribune*, April 1, 1923

"Two More Women Held as Poisoners." *Washington Post*, November 19, 1922.

"Two Poisoned by Candy Given by Mrs. Klimek." *Chicago Daily Tribune*, November 17, 1922.

Wikler, Daniel. "Can We Learn from Eugenics?" *Journal of Medical Ethics* 25, no. 2 (April 1999).

"Woman Bluebeard Calmly Watches Murder Net Close." *Philadelphia Inquirer*, November 19, 1922.

"Woman Convict Who Poisoned Husband, Dies at
    Dwight." *Decatur Daily Review*, November 22, 1936.
"Woman Gives Testimony in Husband Poisoning
    Case." *Minneapolis Morning Tribune*, November 4,
    1922.

Image Credits

CHAPTER 2

Chicago tenement neighborhood, 1920. Courtesy Loc.Gov, Library of Congress.

CHAPTER 3

"Rough on Rats" advertisement, 1901. Courtesy Loc.Gov, Library of Congress.

CHAPTER 5

Photograph of Tillie Klimek, 1922. Courtesy *Chicago Daily Tribune*, March 14, 1923.

CHAPTER 7

Photograph of Lieutenant Malone, Assistant State's Attorney Peden, and Assistant State's Attorney McLaughlin. Courtesy *Chicago Daily Tribune*, March 14, 1923.

CHAPTER 9

Photograph of the trial. Courtesy *Chicago Daily Tribune*, March 14, 1923.

Slingshot Books
Minneapolis

www.slingshotbooks.com